So Great the Devastation

THE 1916 FLOOD IN WESTERN NORTH CAROLINA

Jessica A. Bandel

North Carolina Office of Archives and History
Raleigh
2016

COVER: Alcoa's Narrows Dam at Badin in Stanly County was one of the easternmost points affected by the flood. Marcus Donald Bracey Photograph Collection, North Carolina Office of Archives and History, Raleigh, N.C.

TABLE OF CONTENTS

FOREWORD

Anniversaries are a time for remembrance and reassessment. At the Office of Archives and History much attention goes to milestones such as the sesquicentennial of the Civil War and the centennial of World War I. On the eve of U.S. entry into what was long known as the "Great War," one region of the state experienced exceptional damage and upheaval.

The 1916 flood had a significant impact on western North Carolina and the western Piedmont, leaving unprecedented destruction. Practically all rail lines west of Winston-Salem were affected with scarcely a mile of track between Statesville and Asheville left undamaged. Bridges along the length of the Catawba, Yadkin, and French Broad Rivers were torn from their piers. Hardest hit was agriculture. With topsoil ripped from the fields and waterways literally rerouted, farmers coped with the effects for a generation.

From Marshall to Belmont, Elkin to Bat Cave, the effects were extraordinary. Stories of heroic rescues, crash efforts to rebuild, governmental response, and private philanthropic efforts all document North Carolinians' capacity for resilience. Perhaps most noteworthy were the efforts of neighbor to assist neighbor.

Photographs bring the 1916 flood and its impact back to us a hundred years later. Images document the damage, showing piles of debris, massive mountain slides, and rail ties left swinging. For this publication libraries, historical societies, and individuals have generously responded to our call to share their iconographic resources.

In *So Great the Devastation*, and in the accompanying touring panel exhibit and digital display, Jessica A. Bandel, Research Historian with Archives and History, tells the stories of the 1916 flood in vivid, compelling fashion. The stories and lessons that she recounts herein are ones we today would do well to recall.

Michael Hill, *Supervisor*
Historical Research Office

Communities Affected by the 1916 Flood

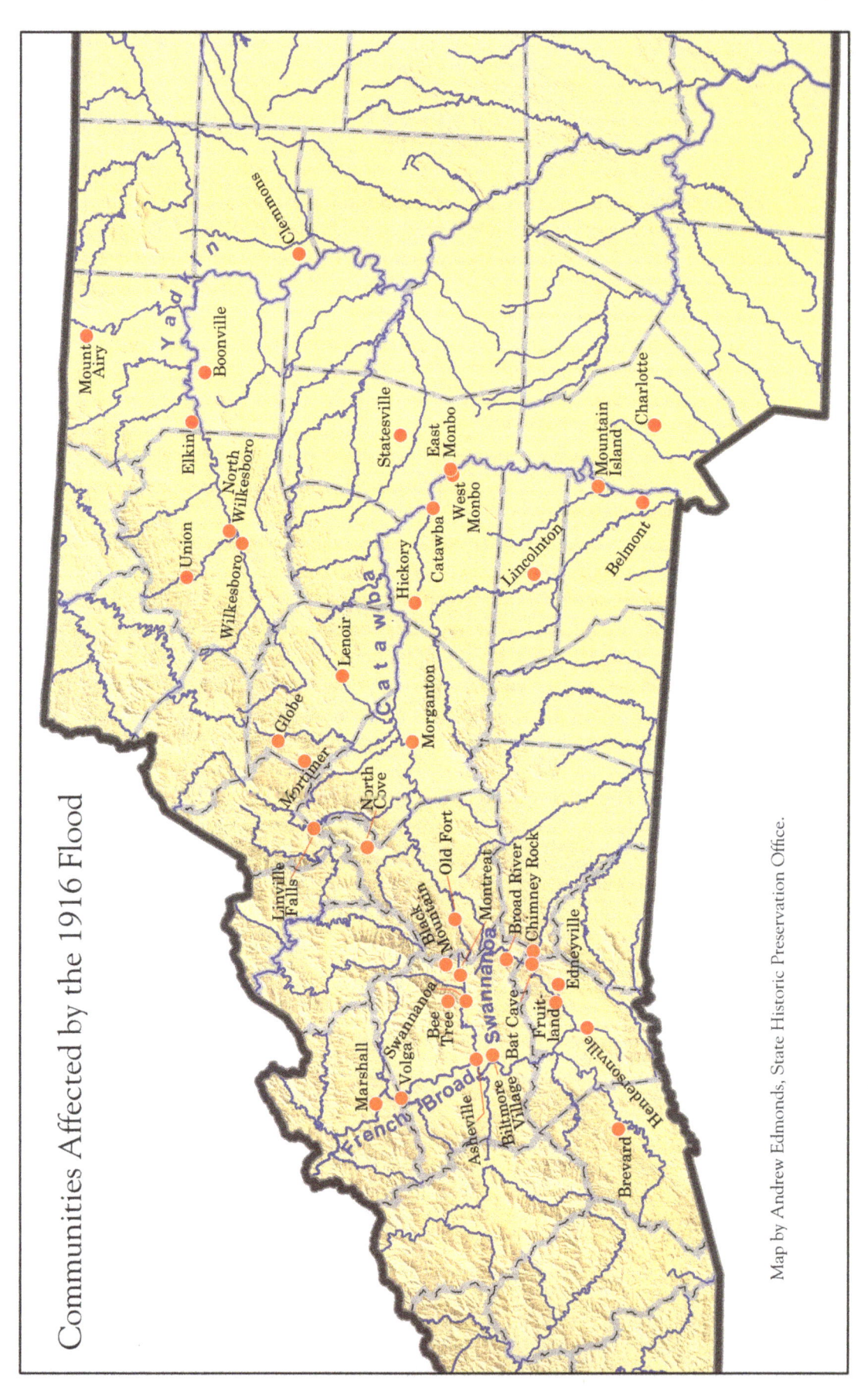

Map by Andrew Edmonds, State Historic Preservation Office.

So Great the Devastation

The 1916 Flood in Western North Carolina

"I shot down into the water like a load of lead," recalled Southern Railway section foreman R. C. Thompson in disbelief. Thompson was one of nineteen Southern workmen who struggled to stabilize a trestle against the raging floodwaters of the Catawba River just east of Belmont, North Carolina, on Sunday, July 16, 1916. Their efforts, however, were no match for Mother Nature, and the trestle succumbed to the force of the Catawba at 5:35 P.M., sending all the Southern's crewmen into the churning currents. From a hospital bed the next day, Thompson calmly recounted his harrowing experience to reporters from the *Charlotte Observer*.

"It seemed like an eternity before I came to the surface again," continued Thompson. Miraculously, he managed to climb aboard a raft with three other colleagues, he told reporters, but the raft was soon lost. The men then faced a long night of swimming, in complete darkness, from treetop to treetop in currents reaching speeds of sixteen miles per hour. Over the roar of the rapids, they heard desperate cries for help and watched for the bodies of fellow crewmen. "I gave more thought to the worry of my wife and little ones than I did of anything else except to getting back to them alive," Thompson offered. At noon the following day, after nineteen hours in the river, Thompson was pulled to safety. He summed up his experience simply: "It was a terrible night."[1]

Though the Belmont trestle disaster proved to be the single greatest loss of life in the 1916 flood, stories equally tragic abound in the river valleys of western North Carolina. In mid-July, a tropical storm pushed inland over western North Carolina from the coast just as the remnants of a tropical depression moved northeast through East Tennessee and the Great Smoky Mountains. The convergence of the two storm systems was catastrophic. Landslides wiped out whole families. Currents ripped babies from their parents' arms. Rivers washed away thousands of jobs. When the water finally receded, at least fifty lay dead, damages totaled in the millions of dollars, and a thick black sludge remained where fields of corn and other grains once stood.[2] The scope of the devastation was almost inconceivable; North Carolina, South Carolina, Georgia, Alabama, Florida, Tennessee, and Mississippi would all need relief aid in the months following the flood.[3] But no state was hit harder than the Old North State.

By the time the tropical storm pushed inland from the coast, it had already been raining in many places in the mountain region for days. The swollen French Broad River had attracted curious Asheville onlookers in the days preceding the tropical storm's arrival, but none could have imagined the extreme magnitude the floodwaters would assume on Saturday, July 15. Beginning at 2:00 P.M. and continuing for twenty-four hours without interruption, an unprecedented twenty-two inches of rain fell in the vicinity of Altapass.[4] Many awoke Sunday morning to a world turned upside down. In the early morning hours, William Thomas Kirkman, a sleepy-eyed four-year-old resident of 1 Swan Street in Biltmore Village, looked out his second-story bedroom window to see "everything . . . covered with water." He went to the stairs next and found the first floor flooded and the family's "player piano floating on its side." Kirkman later recalled that his family wasted no time in evacuating the house as his father carried his family members one-by-one, in waist-deep water, to a horse-drawn carriage that conveyed village residents to higher ground at All Soul's Church.[5]

At the same moment that the Kirkman family escaped to safety, just down the street, the scene was one of chaos and tragedy. The home of James Cornelius Lipe, a master carpenter and superintendent at the Biltmore Estate, stood on the bank of the Swannanoa River near the estate's main entrance. He and his daughter Kathleen were wading from their house towards higher ground in the Village when a sudden rush of water threatened to sweep them off their feet. Lipe helped his daughter and three other young women—Biltmore Hospital nurses Mabel Foister and Charlotte Walker, and Charlotte's younger sister Marion—grab hold of a large tree near the main gate of the estate. None of the young women were strong enough to pull themselves up into the tree, so they tied Kathleen's sweater around the tree trunk providing a grip that all could hold onto. They were stranded, and the water was steadily rising.[6]

Village residents and Biltmore staff gathered on the bank opposite the desperate group to organize rescue parties and provide other assistance as needed. Edith Vanderbilt, owner of the estate, soon arrived on scene and began coordinating relief efforts and recruiting volunteers. Placing all Biltmore resources at the disposal of the rescue party, Mrs. Vanderbilt stood on the edge of the flooded Swannanoa and

The two-story home belonging to the Lipe family, as seen in the image above, sat on the bank of the Swannanoa River in Biltmore. James Lipe and his daughter Kathleen were marooned in a nearby tree with three young women by the rising floodwater. Of the five, only Kathleen survived. From the Durwood Barbour Collection of North Carolina Postcards. Courtesy the North Carolina Collection, Wilson Library, University of North Carolina at Chapel Hill.

passed out hot coffee and sandwiches to the rescuers. She watched helplessly, with the crowd, as her master carpenter and four young women clung to what would be remembered as the "death tree."[7]

After several failed attempts, a volunteer finally managed to reach the tree and all decided that Marion—the youngest—would be the first rescued. But en route back to the shore, she panicked, fought her rescuer, and was quickly swept away. Traumatized by the scene, Charlotte began screaming "Marion! Marion!" and dropped from the tree after her sister. The elder Lipe was the next to go, losing his grip after fighting the flood for six hours. Kathleen later recalled her father muttering "Shucks! Shucks!" in frustration as he was carried away in the current. Mabel reportedly made no sound when she slipped loose. At 2:00 in the afternoon, eight hours after she was stranded in the tree, two Biltmore employees managed to bring Kathleen back to land.[8] Of the Biltmore five, she was the sole survivor.

On the riverfront in Asheville, newspaperman and founder of the state history museum Fred A. Olds stood in awe of the flood's fury as it swept the industrial district. From just above the Southern Railway's concrete viaduct spanning the French Broad, Olds looked on as houses, bridge remnants, machinery, and other debris sped down the river. "Out sailed a house, as if it were a vessel just launched," wrote Olds in astonishment a week later. Olds eyed the house as it sank lower and lower until it "struck the great bridge in a thunder of sound," sending a cloud of plaster dust into the air, a scene Olds likened to an artillery shell striking a house.

From this vantage point, Fred A. Olds looked on helplessly as Walter Trexler and Luther Frazier drowned near the partially submerged cable cars while attempting to deliver provisions to the Glen Rock Hotel. The Southern Railway's depot is the focal point of the image. From *The Floods of July 1916: How the Southern Railway Organization Met an Emergency* (Washington, D.C.: Southern Railway Company, Office of the President, 1917), 57.

Then a loud *crack* rang out, "like that of a three-inch rifle," and a span of a steel bridge upriver from Olds—known as Smith's Bridge—gave way. The remaining spans soon followed, disappearing beneath the water's surface and out of sight.

Olds then travelled upstream to the Southern Railway's depot and described the catastrophic scene unfolding there. The desperate cries of cooped chickens filled the air as Olds and other witnesses looked down from a hilltop just south of the depot. In the railyard to their left, two cars filled with lime smoldered and burst into flames near a car loaded with dynamite. On the city street before them, hundreds of onlookers watched as two men, Luther Frazier and Walter Trexler, attempted to deliver provisions to stranded lodgers at the Glen Rock Hotel opposite the depot. Without warning, their boat capsized. Horrified witnesses looked on as both men fell into the water. "One sank quickly," wrote Olds, while the other struggled briefly before slipping out of sight.

The attention of the crowd then turned to men, women, and children trapped in a nearby tannery.[9] Through a window in the roof of the building, "which seemed about to go every moment," Olds spotted a young mother holding up her baby. The sight threw the men into action, Olds reporting that there were "heroes all about—firemen, policemen, railroadmen, [and] citizens." Without much care for their own safety, the lifesavers cast off in small boats guided by thin ropes and saved every stranded person "while packed hundreds watched, too absorbed to cheer." Following a brief description of the desolate appearance of Biltmore Village, Olds summed up his report with a note on the persevering nature of man saying, quite eloquently, that "Asheville rose to the height of the occasion, just as the river had risen."[9]

Citizens at Belmont would be likewise tested when the Southern Railway trestle spanning the Catawba River gave way Sunday, July 16, at 5:35 P.M., sending nineteen railroad workers into the roaring rapids. Julius White, one of the survivors, later recalled that the trestle dipped down but then rose back up before a loud snapping noise rang out. To White, it sounded like "all the world was coming to an end," and then he hit the water.[10] Hundreds of people, including family and friends of the workers, had gathered along the swollen banks hoping to witness a happy conclusion to the ordeal.[11] Section foreman W. L. Fortune and black railroad workers White and Evans Brown were rescued that evening and early the following morning.[12] Four others—engineer Joseph A. Killian, H. C. Gurley, section master R. C. Thompson, and George C. Kale—swam and clung to debris or trees for nineteen hours before being pulled from the water. Once back on land, the bloodied and bruised survivors broke down in tears and rambled incoherently about their ordeal, completely overwhelmed by the experience.[13]

Two African American men, Gaston County natives Peter Monroe Stowe and Alphonse Leroy Ross, were credited with rescuing four of the seven Belmont survivors and two more men who had attempted an earlier rescue. A week-long drive spear-headed by the *Charlotte Observer* raised $550, all of which was given to Stowe and Ross in recognition of their selfless courage.[14] In an interview with the *Charlotte Observer*, Ross described the rescue saying, "It was hard work pulling against that awful current and we had all we could do to make it across but we had good strong paddles and strong arms and didn't fear about the result." When asked what they intended to do with their reward money, Ross answered that both would buy "a little land" for their families.[15]

In Morganton, Joseph L. Duckworth's store sat two hundred yards from the bank of the Catawba River. By Saturday night, however, the Catawba had begun to creep into the building. Joseph and two of his sons worked feverishly to salvage what they could from the store. When his father and brother left for the safety of higher ground, Alphonso remained behind to gather money and important records.[16] Before he could make his escape, however, a sudden surge of water marooned him. Moving to the second floor, he fabricated a makeshift boat out of lumber, passed it through a window to the water's surface, and carefully tied it off. By morning, however, he found the boat had been swept away. The water continued to rise and poured into the second floor. Climbing to the roof, Alphonso waved frantically to the crowd gathering eight hundred feet away on the swollen river's edge. The onlookers quickly raised a pledge of $1,200 for anyone who would attempt the rescue.[17]

Alphonse Leroy Ross, left, and Peter Monroe Stowe, right, rescued six men from the Catawba River near Belmont on July 16. For their selfless courage, the men shared a $550 purse which had been raised by the *Charlotte Observer*. Image from the *Charlotte Observer*, July 19, 1916.

In 1920, William P. Clark was awarded a bronze medal (like the one pictured here) and $1,000 by the Carnegie Hero Fund for his daring rescue of Alphonso Duckworth from the Catawba River near Morganton. Image of Clark from *The News Herald* (Morganton), June 13, 1918. Image of the bronze medal courtesy the Carnegie Hero Fund Commission.

Only one man stepped forward, twenty-five-year-old William P. Clark. The six-foot-tall, 190-pound Clark put in a half-mile upriver in a fifteen-foot boat around 10:00 A.M. The twenty-mile-per-hour current carried him swiftly to the store, where Duckworth climbed aboard and asked to be taken around to the porch roof so that he could climb into the second floor. Clark obliged. With the records and money in hand, Alphonso returned to the boat, and the two men made their way for shore.[18] When the townsfolk attempted to award Clark the $1,200 purse, he flatly and unflinchingly refused it, saying he would risk his life for his neighbor but not for a sum of money.[19]

Clark's selfless courage would not go unrewarded. C. E. Gregory, a pastor at a Presbyterian church in Morganton, reported Clark's heroism to the Carnegie Hero Fund Commission. Established in 1904 by American industrialist Andrew Carnegie, the fund seeks to recognize those who "risk their lives to an extraordinary degree saving or attempting to save the lives of others."[20] Following a thorough

Joseph L. Duckworth's store in Morganton, seen here immediately following the flood, was completely surrounded and cut off by the Catawba River. His son Alphonso was rescued from the store's roof by William P. Clark. Image from the Estate of Jean Conyers Ervin. It appears courtesy of Picture Burke, a digital photograph preservation project of the Burke County Public Library.

investigation of the rescue, the Carnegie Hero Fund awarded Clark $1,000 and a bronze medal. This recognition Clark humbly accepted.[21]

In Marshall, the seat of Madison County, the French Broad rose steadily through Sunday morning. From the railroad tracks situated between the river bank and Main Street, children passed the time by throwing rocks at trees, boxes, and other debris floating downstream. By noon, water had begun spilling onto Main Street itself, lapping at the foundations of businesses and homes sandwiched between the river and steep hillsides to the north.[22]

Forty-two-year-old Spanish American War veteran James Guthrie worked diligently to carry items from his first floor café to rooms on the second floor hoping to save them from the floodwaters. Two of his sons, Herman and Paul, had stayed near their father's café, joining other kids in throwing rocks at debris, until their excitement turned to concern. Trees and boxes soon gave way to small buildings, livestock, and chickens, all bobbing down the river in the rapids. The sight terrified Paul, the younger of the two at age nine, who then made tracks for their home across the river. Wading through water up to his knees, Paul had barely made it across the wooden bridge when the whole thing collapsed. Perhaps too scared to carry on, he climbed to the top of an old cotton mill for safety and spent the night there.[23]

Herman, age fifteen, remained behind to help his father and his aunt Altha Briggs. When he decided it had grown too dangerous for them to continue, James

The flood changed the course of fifteen-year-old Herman Guthrie's life in ways he could not have imagined. From the banks of the French Broad River in Marshall, Herman watched helplessly as his father James and aunt Altha Briggs were drowned in the floodwaters on that fateful Sunday in July 1916. Traumatized, Herman caught the first train out of Marshall three weeks later and travelled to Norfolk, Virginia, where he lied about his age and secured a job on a ship. A year later, the young man, then sixteen, again lied about his age and joined the 340th Field Artillery, 89th Division, and served in France during World War I. Several mustard gas attacks damaged Herman's airways, necessitating a postwar surgery that removed seventeen small pieces of bone from his nasal passages. He never again lived in Marshall. Image appears courtesy E. Virginia Lapham, Vienna, Va.

told Herman to gather his aunt's bag and escort her home. From atop the detached kitchen, James and Altha watched as Herman collected her things on the second floor. Suddenly, Herman heard his father cry out, "Hurry, the building's moving!" Herman went to the window and saw that the kitchen was slowly sliding off its foundation. He jumped onto some floating lumber and grabbed a small tree to pull himself out of danger. Whirling around to catch sight of the kitchen, he spotted his dad and his aunt still on the roof, floating downriver. Both jumped into the water in an attempt to reach the shore, but the kitchen overturned on them, carrying both below the surface.[24]

In a moment of panic, Herman started back into the water to go after them but was held back by bystanders. Tears streaming down his face, Herman found his brother Delmar and told him what had happened. With both bridges washed out and no way to get word across the river to their mother, the boys went next to their grandparents' house and informed them of the tragic turn of events. Their mother didn't learn of the news until the next day. Standing on the opposite bank of the still swollen river, she carefully read the hand-made sign held up by citizens: "Jim Guthrie and Altha Briggs drowned in flood."[25]

Forty miles south in Hendersonville, rising waters cut the town off from all outside contact. Sixteen-year-old Carl Blythe remembered his mother's anxiety as floodwaters began to creep up near the town's sidewalks and roads. With her home only six blocks from the bank of Mud Creek, she had plenty of cause for concern for both her home and her family, sternly warning Carl to steer clear of the water. Against his mother's wishes, Carl snuck off to a nearby railroad trestle and watched the remains of drowned cattle, sheep, pigs, and dogs speed down the creek and lodge against the trestle.[26] Downtown Hendersonville would be spared, but communities out in the county would not be so fortunate.

Folks out in Bat Cave contended with much more than rising water. Over-saturated soil on the steep mountainsides above their homes posed a great risk for landslides. W. S. Fallis of the State Highway Commission described the "terrific force" of a landslide during an August interview following his survey of the affected area:

I suppose I saw the effects of more than 300 of these slides. They appeared to have started close to the top of the mountains. For a distance of possibly from seventy-five to 200 feet in which they removed everything clear and clean in their paths. . . . Everything movable in their path was swept to the river below. Trees were absolutely denuded of every vestige of bark. Rocks were ground smooth. Buildings were carried away in the irresistible rush.[27]

One such slide, Fallis continued, struck the home of Brown E. Huntley in Bat Cave with tragic consequences. Around 1:00 or 2:00 A.M. Huntley arose from bed to investigate unnerving noises from outside. He first thought it was the sound of water rising from the creek below his house, but as he opened his door to step outside, a wall of rock, mud, and wood slammed against the tiny structure and pushed it—and his family—right into the clutches of the flood. Huntley lost his twenty-nine-year-old wife, Belle, and their two adopted children, Bonnie and Fred Hill, ages seven and eleven.[28]

To the west in Brevard, Martha Sentell and her five-year-old daughter Susan met similar fates when their home on the Davidson River was struck by a landslide. Another daughter sustained serious bruises but recovered fully.[29] On the Little River in northern Alexander County, a landslide crashed down on the home of Lonas and Lillie Russell. The couple managed to escape the house with a child each, but their three oldest children—Jennie, Louis, and John, ages 6, 7, & 9—were swept away in the slide. John's body was never recovered.[30] The flood claimed lives in other ways too. At least four Burke County residents, including three-month-old twins, died from medical conditions or illnesses without receiving medical care because doctors could not reach them on account of high water.[31] Forty-six-year-old Sherman McKinney was killed when floodwaters undermined a chimney's stability, causing it to fall on him.[32]

The Aftermath

The flood washed out fills, or earthen supports for railroad tracks, leaving tracks suspended mid-air in many places. Five daring men posed for this picture shortly after the flood on a stretch of suspended track between Old Fort and Ridgecrest. From *The Floods of July 1916*, 68.

As the water receded, an apocalyptic landscape emerged where once bustling communities and valley farms had stood. Homes had either simply vanished or were found some distance from their foundations. Men shoveled thick black mud from their houses and assessed structural damage while their wives attempted to wash the dirt from salvaged linens and housewares in the still-muddy streams. A "slick, black ooze" and piles of debris remained where floodwaters had raged, filling the air with a pungent odor. Townsfolk improvised plank-board sidewalks to keep from being mired in the mud and muck. Mail and paper routes, telegraph lines, roads, and railroads—most contemporary means of communication and transportation—had all been severed.[33] In Globe, two entire cemeteries completely disappeared.[34] In churches across the region, preachers questioned the meaning of the flood, searching for purpose in the devastation and loss of life.[35]

Standing water and debris piles posed major threats as ideal breeding grounds for mosquitos and flies, causing concern for outbreaks of malaria and other mosquito-borne diseases. Health officials advised citizens to install screens on windows and doors to keep potentially deadly insects out of their living spaces. State and county health officials also warned residents of the dangers of contaminated water, urging all those affected to boil drinking water, to clean and flush their wells, and to get typhoid vaccinations.[36] Free vaccinations provided by the State Board of Health were administered by county health superintendents.[37] McDowell County health superintendent Gaston B. Justice went a step further by asking residents to submit water samples from their wells for analysis.[38]

"You have to realize this was a different time," recalled Samuel J. Bryson of Hendersonville on the 70th anniversary of the flood. "Electricity was just starting. There were hardly any cars. No radio, no plumbing. We had never experienced anything like this before."[39] Statewide property loss estimates measured in the millions—anywhere between $10,000,000 and $25,000,000.[40] Many families were left completely destitute, but no one seemed harder hit than the farmer. "Their all has been swept away in a night," announced Gov. Locke Craig. "In hundreds of instances everything that the tenant-farmer had was lost—his stock, his house, his furniture, his crop."[41] In many places, the land itself was washed away. Along the Yadkin River from Elkin to the Forsyth County line, a distance of thirty-three miles, the topsoil was completely stripped, leaving "nothing but a barren plain."[42]

Many survivors returned to their homes only to find that they were complete losses. All manner of debris can be found washed up against the house in this image. The exact location of the scene is unknown. Courtesy of the Lincoln County Historical Association.

Citizens in Clemmons, a small town outside of Winston-Salem, petitioned the governor on behalf of their friend W. H. Bonner. Bonner, they wrote, had lost his entire crop to the Yadkin River and was responsible for the care of his twelve-year-old daughter, his cancer-stricken father, and an aged aunt. "He . . . is in serious need of outside aid," the brief note concluded.[43] Attorney F. W. Thomas appealed to the relief committee in regards to a friend of his—"a poor farmer in Henderson County"—who lost his crop valued at $125. "While this is not a large sum," Thomas wrote, "it is big for him. . . . He is deserving of relief, and if anything can be done for him, I would be glad."[44] C. M. Doyle, secretary of the relief committee, telegraphed fellow committee member J. W. Bailey from Transylvania County to report that a large number of tenant farmers had lost their entire crops and that several families had "lost everything."[45]

A report on conditions in Elkin identified another problem that would affect many farmers throughout the flood district. The extensive loss of corn, oats, grasses, and other field crops used as silage left farmers incapable of feeding their livestock through the winter.[46] Those who came out of the flood with their livestock intact faced the new problem of finding a way to feed and maintain them. From Gaston County, a local relief committee reported that many farmers were selling off their surviving livestock "at a sacrifice" because they could no longer care for them. "Of course we cannot replace these losses, but can you not assist us in giving these good citizens some relief?" the committee asked.[47]

Farmers were the hardest hit. In many instances, the flood took not only a farmer's house, but his crop and outbuildings as well. This photograph depicts the loss of an entire field of corn as the North Fork of the Catawba River cut a new channel right across this farmer's property in Linville Falls. From the Frank W. Bicknell Photograph Collection, North Carolina Office of Archives and History, Raleigh, N.C.

Relief, Recovery, and Reconstruction

Despite the hardships, generosity pervaded many mountain communities. One man who lost "everything he had—home, land, and stock—except one crib of corn" shared that last crib with neighbors in need.[48] While such neighborly generosity went a long way in the days immediately following the flood, it became immediately apparent to state and federal officials that relief efforts would have to be large in scope, well-coordinated, and swiftly and effectively executed. To meet this end, Governor Craig appointed a Committee of General Relief and tasked its members with the coordination of state relief efforts and the collection and distribution of donations.[49]

On the Federal side, financial relief aid was buoyed by a $540,000 appropriation, which was to be distributed to the affected states on the basis of need. Of this amount, $80,000 was set aside to fund a seed distribution program stewarded by the Department of Agriculture. Over one million pounds of field seed (millet, oats, buckwheat, soybeans, etc.) and close to 25,000 pounds of vegetable seed (turnips, kale, spinach, beets, collards, etc.) were distributed in the affected states.[50] Seeds were acquired by flood sufferers through their county demonstration agents.[51] In addition to funding, the federal government sent representatives to meet with state officials to coordinate relief efforts. Gilbert A. Youngberg, Army Corps of Engineers, and J. A. Evans, Department of Agriculture, travelled to Raleigh to inform the committee and the governor on Federal aid and relief plans.[52]

By August 10, the state relief committee had accrued $75,000 in funds from donors across the state and nation, including a $500 contribution by Ford Motor Company.[53] Newspapers often acted as the official collection bodies, advertising the donors' names and amounts given so as to encourage more gifts. Donations accrued from local efforts as well. The Crescent Theater in Statesville aired a "special picture for the benefit" of those in need of aid, charging between five and ten cents for admission. "The management will bear all expenses and [will] give every cent of the proceeds to the fund for the flood sufferers," announced the theater.[54] Towns across the region held similar fundraisers, offering to donate the admission to plays, movies, concerts, and picnics to flood relief funds.

Local businesses provided help in other ways, extending discounts to citizens who were hard hit by the flood. In Lenoir, the Henkel-Deal Company offered a steep thirty-three percent discount on Nissen Wagons in the hopes of helping flood sufferers back onto their feet.[55] Kirksey & Company in Morganton placed an advertisement in the *News-Herald* empathizing with flood victims. "We deeply sympathize," began the ad in bold letters, "with all those who have lost in the recent flood on the Catawba and Johns rivers, and, to show that we mean more than mere words in expressing our sympathy . . . we will freely give a discount of 10 per cent on your bill."[56] Banks, groceries, hardware stores, and other Main Street establishments across the flood district offered similar discounts or assistance.

Despite the flurry of giving, financial assistance was slow to reach affected areas immediately following the flood as the state relief committee members worked to inventory the damage. Their reports revealed extensive destruction across the region. In McDowell County alone, an August 10 survey enumerated 210 families as completely destitute and 500 families as partially destitute, but only 121 families as having received relief aid.[57] In Surry County, at least 300 people needed assistance.[58] State relief committee chairman C. E. Brooks warned Governor Craig via telegram that "conditions [are] more serious than first reported" in Hendersonville and found twenty-five families "in destitute circumstances."[59] A citizen from Boonville (Yadkin County) warned the committee that the destruction in his section was worse than originally thought and reported fifty families in desperate need of aid.[60] A Marshall citizen pleaded with the governor via telegram for "money to put the town in a sanitary condition at once."[61]

"The more we investigate the loss in this section[,] the worse we find it," reported banker Alex Chatham from Elkin.[62] A followup report on the state of the town by Mount Airy attorney W. F. Carter revealed a loss of twenty-five houses. "The occupants for the most part were laborers," continued Carter, "and everything they had was washed away in the houses, leaving them nothing and out of employment and they are in need of immediate help." Additionally, extensive damage to the Chatham Manufacturing Company's property in Elkin left 150 citizens out of work.[63] In Ashe County, citizens reported similar destruction, indicating that it was "almost impossible" to describe "the damage and havoc that has been wrought in our county by the recent flood." Homes, stores, mills, barns, bridges, gardens, and crops were all named as casualties of the high water. Many people were left without even a change of clothes.[64]

Relief committee member A. M. Scales reported from the Yadkin River Valley that the families in the most desperate need were the ones who, prior to the flood, had lived hand-to-mouth. "Most of these people are indebted to the supply merchant and to the landlord," Scales summarized. Businessmen and large-scale landowners, though hard hit, "would scorn to receive any aid" and were "able to stand the loss." Scales was unable even to survey the damage in Ashe and Alleghany Counties due to the devastation. "The roads and bridges were washed away to such an extent that I was advised not to attempt this trip," Scales wrote. He concluded his letter by recommending that the responsibility of relief aid

Flood sufferers found support in a variety of places. Local businesses often offered steep discounts to those who were hard hit by the flood while others donated a portion of ticket sales to relief funds. Henkel-Deal Company ad from the *Lenoir News*, August 4, 1916. Galax Theatre ad from the *Asheville Citizen*, July 20, 1916.

distribution be carried out by local committees "as the local men know the people and are more familiar with their needs and with what they have lost."[65]

In regards to infrastructure damage, mill and lumber towns, typically situated on rivers, were among the hardest hit. In Iredell County, the cotton mill at West Monbo on the Catawba River was "washed as completely away as though somebody had come along with an eraser and blotted it from the landscape." Its sister mill across the river at East Monbo was seriously damaged. Total losses at both Monbo mills were estimated between $150,000 and $175,000. The greatest financial loss, however, was incurred by Armon Manufacturing Company, whose mills on Mountain Island outside of Mount Holly in Gaston County were also swept away.

"It is impossible to detect any trace of the two mills," remarked one observer. Several dwellings that housed the mills' laborers and their families were also destroyed. Armon's losses totaled $250,000.[66] At Mortimer, in Caldwell County, the W. M. Ritter Lumber Company was hard hit, losing thirty-two houses, twenty to twenty-five miles of railway and tram-lines, and a supply house. A commissary, theater, school, and offices were damaged but deemed salvageable.[67] Not only were blue collar laborers across the flood district out of work, in many cases, they were also left homeless.

As they awaited the aid, farmers, mill workers, and other laborers left jobless in the wake of the flood sought temporary employment in the recovery effort, especially with railroad construction crews. Southern Railway construction camps sprang up throughout the region, each camp accommodating anywhere from ten to three hundred men. The camps were supplied with potable water, canned goods, showers, and tents. Health officials hired by the railroad companies worked to vaccinate the men for typhoid and to prevent outbreaks of lice and infectious

The Armon Manufacturing Company mill complex on Mountain Island—consisting of a five-story, brick cotton mill; a warehouse and 1,000 bales of cotton; and dwellings for the labor force—was completely swept away, leaving nothing but the island's rocky surface. The mill was situated on the Catawba River, approximately four miles north of Mount Holly in Gaston County. Courtesy of the Lincoln County Historical Association.

diseases.[68] As a result, only a few cases of fever and pneumonia were reported. Men from Virginia and the Carolinas responded overwhelmingly to the promise of room, board, and the $1.50 per day wage.[69] By August 17, between 2,000 and 2,500 men were at work—night and day—on the twelve-mile stretch of the Southern Railway between Old Fort and Ridgecrest alone, turning small-town Old Fort into a "veritable human bee hive."[70]

Though many families were in immediate need of food, clothing, and shelter, the inaccessibility of roads and railroads hampered relief efforts.[71] In McDowell County, thirty-eight bridges were total losses and one was heavily damaged. Fifty percent of public and county roads there were lost.[72] In some portions of Caldwell County, residents were reported to have had "no way of egress or ingress, their only way of travel is by foot." Their road system was in such a state of disrepair that county officials appropriated $50,000 for reconstruction but sought additional funding from the state highway department.[73] Hendersonville residents seeking to deliver aid to Bat Cave and Chimney Rock could only go as far as Edneyville by

Work commenced immediately following the flood to repair or reconstruct damaged roads and railroads. As seen above, a crew employed by the Southern Railway works to clear debris from the mouth of Lick Log Tunnel in McDowell County. From *The Floods of July 1916*, 60.

car, the road being washed out beyond that point.[74] Roads and bridges all over the region were lost or seriously damaged. Upon concluding a tour of the flood district, state highway engineer W. S. Fallis estimated total damage to the road system at $500,000 and the total cost of lost bridges at $1,000,000.[75]

Residents of North Cove and Broad River in McDowell County petitioned the governor via telegram on August 10 for employment rebuilding their devastated road system. "We are cut off from markets and are packing in supplies from Black Mountain," wrote Broad River residents. "Loss of crops and lands is great," they continued, "but we need most of all roads and as promptly as possible." In their concluding line, the group of twenty-two promised the governor "all who are able will help with team and labor."[76] The North Cove residents echoed the sentiment of their neighbors' telegram saying that they had "suffered great loss of houses livestock land and crops" and asked "for aid to build roads." Driving home the level of desperation in their community, the men declared that they could not "even thresh what wheat was saved." "Road funds," they added, "will give self help[,] restore roads and give opportunity to work in forest products."[77]

On that same day, Durham industrialist and relief committee member Julian Carr telegraphed Governor Craig from Hickory recommending just such a labor relief program for the district encompassing McDowell, Burke, Iredell, Caldwell, Wilkes, Ashe, and Catawba Counties. "What I most apprehend is that some of these fine North Carolina citizens may become discouraged and want to migrate," Carr cautioned. "If possible," Carr continued, "work such as road building [and] repairing bridges should begin in the district in the very near future[.] Otherwise a loss to the state greater than occasioned by the flood is likely to occur."[78] Such a program was already in effect in Transylvania County, where 250 residents had applied for and received employment repairing the roads in the county.[79] In late August, the relief committee rolled out just such a program, offering relief aid in the form of pay for laborers engaged in repairing the roads. For an eight-hour day, a man could earn one dollar. A man with a team could earn $2.50 for the same amount of time worked. Interested parties were required to apply for a position, applications being submitted to C. M. Doyle of the relief committee.

With nearly every working man in the region mobilized, many reconstruction projects were completed in the months following the flood. On August 25, after five weeks in the dark, light and power returned to McDowell County where residents "hailed" its return with "great delight."[80] Higher priority projects were completed within days of the flood. When the Southern Power Company's plant at Great Falls, South Carolina, succumbed to the floodwaters, severing power to Charlotte and textile plants in the Piedmont, officials immediately took to the telegraph wires to find another power source. Power surged back into the city and surrounding area mere hours after it first failed, travelling a circuitous route of more than 600 miles from a power station at Tallulah Falls, Georgia.[81] The work crews of the Southern Railway responded with the same zeal and energy, restoring full service on most of their lines by September.[82] Other projects, however, took years. It was not until April 1919 that Mecklenburg County completed the reconstruction of the last of four key bridges lost in the flood.[83]

"The old mill and the community known as Mountain Island are no longer," wrote a journalist for the *Gastonia Gazette* in February 1955. The raging floodwaters of the Catawba River had completely wiped the five-story cotton mill and related dwelling houses from the map in July 1916, leaving the laborers and their families little choice but to leave the immediate area, many settling elsewhere permanently. Beginning in 1922, however, the former employees and residents of Mountain Island endeavored to gather annually on the second Sunday of September to reconnect with family and friends, share stories, and keep the memory of their vanished community alive. They carried on the tradition well into the 1970s, perhaps beyond. "The mill today is gone, and so is the community," continued the 1955 article, "but the waters which washed them away could not dampen the spirit of loyalty . . . of those who once lived and worked and had fellowship there."[84]

In their reunions, the Mountain Island residents surely found comfort and healing from their terrifying experiences and life-altering losses. Other flood survivors, however, carried the scars of that experience with them for the rest of their lives. William Thomas Kirkman, the four-year old who survived the flooding in Biltmore Village that claimed four lives, later recalled the experience left him with a fear of water as a child. "Not understanding the cause," Kirkman confessed, "Mother later said that each time bath water was running I called out 'another flood.' "[85] Fuschia Gregg Stevens was a child living with her family in the Bee Tree community, outside Swannanoa, when the flood occurred and shared similar fears. The memories of that fateful weekend haunted her for the rest of her life. "For a while I got scared every time it sprinkled rain," Stevens later recalled. "Now I'm better. But it's the kind of experience you never quite get over."[86] Many survivors undoubtedly felt the same.

Endnotes

1. "Chief Thoughts of Rescued Bridge Victim for Family Across the Raging Catawba," *Charlotte Observer*, July 18, 1916; "Rescuers Battle for Hours to Save Six in Treetops on Catawba," *Charlotte Observer*, July 18, 1916.

2. Contemporary newspapers reported death totals exceeding eighty, but a thorough survey of death certificates from all counties in the western portion of the state revealed forty-two deaths. Another nine are accounted for in the Southern Railway's publication *The Floods of July 1916: How the Southern Railway Organization Met an Emergency* and relevant newspaper articles.

3. *Annual Reports of the Department of Agriculture, For the Year Ended June 30, 1917* (Washington, D.C.: Government Printing Office, 1918), 148.

4. W. M. Bell, *The North Carolina Flood: July 14, 15, 16, 1916* (Charlotte: W. M. Bell, 1916), 16.

5. William Thomas Kirkman, "The Autobiography of William Thomas Kirkman," undated, William T. Kirkman Photograph Collection, D. H. Ramsey Library, Special Collections, UNC Asheville, Asheville.

6. Betty Carter Brock, "The Lipe Family in the 1916 Flood," in *The Heritage of Old Buncombe County*, 2 vols. (Winston-Salem: Hunter Publishing Co., 1981), 2:238–239.

7. Bell, 23.

8. Brock, "The Lipe Family in the 1916 Flood," *Heritage of Old Buncombe County*, 2:238–239; Bell, 17.

9. "Marooned in Asheville, N.C.: Story of the Great Flood," *Greensboro Daily News*, July 23, 1916.

10. "Graphic Story of Night in the Water Given by Negro Julius White to News," *Charlotte News*, July 21, 1916.

11. "Catawba Sweeps Ruin in its Furious Rush," *Charlotte News*, July 17, 1916.

12. "Three More Men Rescued from the River," *Charlotte News*, July 18, 1916.

13. "Catawba Sweeps Ruin in its Furious Rush," *Charlotte News*, July 17, 1916; "Will More Men Be Saved?" *Charlotte News*, July 18, 1916.

14. Bell, 12.

15. "Two Negroes, Who Rescued Six White Flood Victims, Tell of Their Exploit," *Charlotte Observer*, July 19, 1916.

16. Newspapers reported that Alphonso remained behind to rescue some chickens on the second flood, but it is far more likely that he risked his life to save items of great importance. Additionally, it is likely that the reminiscences of two of Alphonso's descendants are far more reliable than the sensational reports of contemporary newspaper editors. Bessie Duckworth Turner and Nellie Duckworth Giles, "Fons Tilmond Duckworth," in *The Heritage of Burke County*, 2 vols. (Morganton, NC: Burke County Historical Society), 1:160.

17. "Daring Rescue from Top of Store Building—Real Heroism Shown," *News-Herald* (Morganton), July 18, 1916.

18. Turner and Giles, "Fons Tilmond Duckworth," *Heritage of Burke County*, 1:160; "Daring Rescue from Top of Store Building—Real Heroism Shown," *News-Herald* (Morganton), July 18, 1916.

19. Elizabeth Avery, "A Burke County Hero of the 1916 Flood," Burke County Public Library, Morganton.

20. "Carnegie Hero Fund Commission Home Page," *Carnegie Hero Fund Commission*, accessed September 18, 2015, www.carnegiehero.org/

21. It is worthy of note of William Clark that he would go on to become the first volunteer from Burke County to enlist following the United States' declaration of war during World War I. In 1918, during the height of the so called Spanish Flu epidemic, Clark contracted influenza while stationed at a military camp, beginning eight long years of invalidism. He would succumb to chronic tuberculosis while a patient at the military hospital at Oteen on April 28, 1925. He was thirty-three years old. "Carnegie Hero Award to Morganton Man," *News-Herald* (Morganton), November 4, 1920.

22. Fay Guthrie Owen, "Guthrie," in *Madison County Heritage*, 2 vols. (Waynesville, NC: Madison County Heritage Book Committee, 1994), 1: 22–23.

23. Owen, "Guthrie," in *Madison County Heritage*, 1: 22–23.

24. Owen, "Guthrie," in *Madison County Heritage*, 1: 22–23.

25. In a 1978 interview with his niece E. Virginia Lapham, Herman recalled being with his mother across the river when she learned of the discovery of the remains of her husband and sister. In the audio recording, Herman also stated that the townsfolk wrote simply "man found" and "woman found" on the blackboard, not the names of his father and aunt. This version of the story varies slightly from Herman's written recollections cited here.

26. "Residents Remember Flood of 1916," *Times-News* (Hendersonville), July 16, 1986.

27. "Not in 100 Years will Bat Cave Catastrophe be again Possible," *French Broad Hustler* (Hendersonville), August 3, 1916.

28. "Father Tells of Loss of Wife and Children," *French Broad Hustler* (Hendersonville), August 3, 1916.

29. "Mrs. Caldwell Sentell and Her Daughter Lost Lives in Storm," *Brevard News*, July 21, 1916.

30. "Several are Drowned," *Mountain Scout* (Taylorsville), July 26, 1916; "News from Northern Alexander," *Mountain Scout* (Taylorsville), July 19, 1916; "Two Bodies Recovered," *Mountain Scout* (Taylorsville), July 26, 1916.

31. Anna H. Dellinger, of Linville, died July 13 of an unknown cause at age 22. Charlie Cooper, of the same community, died on July 20 at age 7. Three-month-old twins Lillie and Londa McGee experienced vomiting and diarrhea in the twenty-four hours preceding their deaths. All four death certificates note that doctors could not reach the patients due to flooding. All were buried at Oak Grove Church in Nebo. If residents in other counties died without receiving medical care on account of the flood, it was not so noted on their death certificates. *North Carolina Death Certificates (Burke County), 1909–1976*, (Provo, UT, USA: Ancestry.com Operations Inc, 2007), accessed June 2, 2015, ancestry.com.

32. *North Carolina Death Certificates (McDowell County), 1909–1976*, (Provo, UT, USA: Ancestry.com Operations Inc, 2007), accessed June 2, 2015, ancestry.com.

33. "Wonderful Work of Recuperation," *Charlotte News*, July 25, 1916; "Western Union Service," *Charlotte News*, July 19, 1916.

34. "Caldwell County Worse Hit Than it was First Thought," *Charlotte News*, July 26, 1916.

35. "Does God Send Destruction?: A Lesson from the Flood," *Charlotte News*, July 22, 1916. The sermon was to be held at St. Peter's Episcopal Church in Charlotte on Sunday, July 23.

36. "To Check Spread of Typhoid Boil Water, Get Vaccinated," *Marion Progress*, August 10, 1916.

37. "Aftermath of Floods," *Carolina Watchman* (Salisbury), July 26, 1916.

38. *Marion Progress*, August 3, 1916.

39. "Residents Remember Flood of 1916," *Times-News* (Hendersonville), July 16, 1986.

40. "Estimate Made of Total Damage from Big Floods," *Charlotte Observer*, July 22, 1916.

41. May F. Jones, ed., *Public Letters and Papers of Locke Craig: Governor of North Carolina, 1913–1917* (Raleigh: Edwards & Broughton Printing Company, 1916), 241.

42. W. F. Carter to Gov. Locke Craig, August 1, 1916, Locke Craig Papers, Governor's Papers, State Archives, Office of Archives and History, Raleigh.

43. J. W. Willis et al., to Gov. Locke Craig, July 29, 1916, Locke Craig Papers, Governor's Papers.

44. F. W. Thomas to B. W. Kilgore, August 3, 1916, Locke Craig Papers, Governor's Papers.

45. C. M. Doyle to J. W. Bailey, telegram, undated, Locke Craig Papers, Governor's Papers.

46. W. F. Carter to Gov. Locke Craig, August 1, 1916, Locke Craig Papers, Governor's Papers.

47. S. L. Cathey to Gov. Locke Craig, August 28, 1916, Locke Craig Papers, Governor's Papers.

48. Jones, ed., *Letters and Papers of Locke Craig*, 241.

49. Jones, ed., *Letters and Papers of Locke Craig*, 233–234.

50. *Annual Reports of the Department of Agriculture, For the Year Ended June 30, 1917* (Washington, DC: Government Printing Office, 1918), 148.

51. *Marion Progress*, August 31, 1916.

52. Jones, ed., *Letters and Papers of Locke Craig*, 237.

53. *Charlotte News*, July 28, 1916; Jones, ed., *Letters and Papers of Locke Craig*, 236.

54. "Brief Items Local News," *Statesville Landmark*, August 1, 1916.

55. "Benefit Flood Sufferers" advertisement, *Lenoir News*, August 4, 1916.

56. "We Deeply Sympathize," *News-Herald* (Morganton), July 18, 1916.

57. *Marion Progress*, August 10, 1916.

58. W. F. Carter to Gov. Locke Craig, August 1, 1916, Locke Craig Papers, Governor's Papers.

59. C. E. Brooks to Gov. Locke Craig, telegram, August 8, 1916, Locke Craig Papers, Governor's Papers.

60. T. L. Hayes to A. M. Scales, August 8, 1916, Locke Craig Papers, Governor's Papers.

61. N. B. McDevitt to Gov. Locke Craig, telegram, August 12, 1916, Locke Craig Papers, Governor's Papers.

62. *[Illegible]* to A. M. Scales, August 5, 1916, Locke Craig Papers, Governor's Papers.

63. W. F. Carter to Gov. Locke Craig, August 1, 1916, Locke Craig Papers, Governor's Papers.

64. Unknown author to R. M. Hanes, August 9, 1916, Locke Craig Papers, Governor's Papers.

65. A. M. Scales to Gov. Locke Craig, August 5, 1916, Locke Craig Papers, Governor's Papers.

66. "Losses Sustained by Cotton Mills Not Staggering," *Charlotte Observer*, July 20, 1916.

67. "Caldwell County Worse Hit Than it was First Thought," *Charlotte News*, July 26, 1916.

68. *Marion Progress*, August 3, 1916

69. "No Loafers in Hickory is Dictum," *Hickory Daily Record*, July 19, 1916; "Bridgemen from all Sections," *Charlotte News*, July 19, 1916.

70. "2,000 Men at Work." *Marion Progress*, August 24, 1916.

71. *Marion Progress*, August 3, 1916.

72. *Marion Progress*, August 10, 1916.

73. M. N. Hanshaw to Gov. Locke Craig, telegram, August 1, 1916, Locke Craig Papers, Governor's Papers.

74. This fact didn't deter the good samaritans, however, as they completed the trek by foot. "Residents Remember Flood of 1916," *Times-News* (Hendersonville), July 16, 1986.

75. "Estimate Bridge Damage is Million," *Sylvan Valley News* (Brevard), August 11, 1916.

76. T. B. Ledbetter et al., to Gov. Locke Craig, telegram, August 10, 1916, Locke Craig Papers, Governor's Papers.

77. J. C. Conley et al., to Gov. Locke Craig, telegram, August 10, 1916, Locke Craig Papers, Governor's Papers.

78. Julian Carr to Gov. Locke Craig, telegram, August 10, 1916, Locke Craig Papers, Governor's Papers.

79. "250 Men Receive Road Relief Funds," *Sylvan Valley News* (Brevard), August 25, 1916.

80. *Marion Progress*, August 31, 1916.

81. "Record Breaking Feat Brings Power over Six Hundred Miles from Georgia," *Charlotte News*, July 18, 1916.

82. *The Floods of July 1916: How the Southern Railway Organization Met an Emergency* (Washington, D.C.: Southern Railway Company, Office of the President, 1917), 57.

83. "New Rozzelle's Ferry Bridge Will Be Opened," *Charlotte Observer*, April 4, 1919.

84. "Old Mountain Island Mill Vanished in 1916 Flood; Made Rebel Blankets," *Gastonia Gazette*, February 21, 1921; "Mt. Island Homecoming Slated Sunday," *Gastonia Gazette*, September 5, 1957; "Annual Mountain Island Homecoming Set Sunday," *Gastonia Gazette*, September 9, 1955.

85. Kirkman, "Autobiography," William T. Kirkman Photograph Collection.

86. *Asheville Times*, July 17, 1980.

North Carolina Victims of the 1916 Flood

Town, County	Age	Name
Asheville, Buncombe County	26	Frazier, Luther I.
	25	Trexler, Walter A.
Bat Cave, Henderson County	8	Hill, Bonnie
	11	Hill, Fred
	14	Hill, Stacy
	28	Huntley, Belle
Belmont, Gaston County	22	Adams, Sloan
	Unknown	Ashwood, Tom
	Unknown	Barbee, Corum S.
	Unknown	Davy, Tom
	30	Ferguson, Will
	33	Gordon, John Neacy
	33	Griffin, H. P.
	Unknown	Heath, Daniel
	Unknown	Kluttz, Walter Cicero
	Unknown	Scott, Andrew
Biltmore Village, Buncombe County	24	Foister, Mabel Hortense
	62	Lipe, James Cornelius
	25	Walker, Charlotte M.
	16	Walker, Marion Emma
Brevard, Transylvania County	37	Heath, John Jr.
	36	Sentell, Martha
	5	Sentell, Susan Avo
Charlotte, Mecklenburg County	33	Brotherton, William Jr.
Chimney Rock, Rutherford County	7	Grant, Ruth
	Unknown	Hall, M. B.
	17	Lewis, Dexter
Fruitland, Henderson County	77	Connor, Isaac W.
	11 months	Freeman, Catherine

North Carolina Victims of the 1916 Flood

Town, County	Age	Name
Globe, Caldwell County	67	Moore, Lizzie Denny
Hickory, Catawba County	19	Pope, John Augustus
Johns River, Caldwell County	3	Clark, Jennie A.
	22	Shoemaker, Florence Elizabeth
	3	Shoemaker, Ralph Vernon
Little River, Alexander County	7	Russell, Doctor Louis
	6	Russell, Jennie May
	9	Russell, John Perry
Marshall, Madison County	Unknown	Briggs, Altha C.
	44	Guthrie, James H.
North Cove, McDowell County	2	Gillespie, Katie Ann
	6	McGee, Annie
	3	McGee, Brison
	18	McGee, Nora Edna
	46	McKinney, Sherman
Union, Wilkes County	44	Perry, Jonathan
Volga, Buncombe County	Unknown	Collins, Polly
	Unknown	Collins, Sue
Walnut Grove, Wilkes County	25	Caudill, Alice
	10	Caudill, Cornelius
	46	Jonas, Wady

Contemporary newspapers reported death totals exceeding eighty, but a survey of multiple sources, including death certificates, revealed a total of fifty persons lost. Information compiled from *North Carolina Death Certificates* (multiple counties), 1909–1976, (Provo, UT, USA: Ancestry.com Operations Inc., 2007), accessed June 2, 2015, ancestry.com; *The Floods of July 1916: How the Southern Railway Organization Met an Emergency* (Washington, D.C.: Southern Railway Company, Office of the President, 1917), 131; "Revised Death List," *Asheville-Citizen Times*, July 20, 1916.

OPPOSITE PAGE: Taken from the west bank of the French Broad River, this photograph shows Smith's Bridge (the truss bridge found near the center of the image) before it collapsed. The flooded dwellings of West Asheville residents appear in the foreground. Courtesy North Carolina Collection, Pack Memorial Library, Asheville, North Carolina.

Photographic Essay

Incredibly, this photograph of the Southern Railway's depot in Elkin was taken after the floodwaters had already fallen three feet. Elkin's industrial district was hard hit by the flood, as was an African American community that was "completely wiped out." From *The Floods of July 1916: How the Southern Railway Organization Met an Emergency* (Washington, D.C.: Southern Railway Company, Office of the President, 1917), 77.

BELOW: At Montreat, Flat Creek—with an estimated velocity of nineteen feet per second—easily washed away bridges and the wooden dam that formed Lake Susan. The garage pictured in this image sat below the dam and was flooded. Courtesy North Carolina Collection, Pack Memorial Library, Asheville, North Carolina.

In the vicinity of Black Mountain, the floodwaters of the Swannanoa River flowed at thirteen feet per second, easily washing away a bridge that connected both sides of town. The Perley & Crockett Company logging operation on Mount Mitchell sustained a $2,000 loss during the flood, but the heaviest damage in the area was suffered by the Southern Railway. Torrents of water rushing down the mountainsides washed out the track in many places on the route stretching from Black Mountain to Asheville. Damage to personal property in the small village seems to have been limited to the few dwellings located along Flat Creek. In this photograph, floodwaters encroach on a small, ramshackle house in Black Mountain. Courtesy of the Swannanoa Valley Museum.

Local residents gather at the remains of the Farmer's Union store and a blacksmith shop at the intersection of Whitson Avenue and Old U.S. Highway 70 in Swannanoa. Three houses and the Whitson Avenue bridge, all in the immediate area in which this scene was captured, were also lost. Courtesy of the Swannanoa Valley Museum.

BACKGROUND: This photograph captures the flooded Catawba River surrounding the Duckworth store in Morganton. William P. Clark received a bronze medal and a $1,000 cash reward for rescuing Alphonso Duckworth from the store during the height of the flood. Image from the Estate of Jean Conyers Ervin. It appears courtesy of Picture Burke, a digital photograph preservation project of the Burke County Public Library.

The flooded Yadkin River severely damaged Alcoa's Narrows Dam construction site at Badin, North Carolina, washing away equipment and construction materials. Marcus Donald Bracey Photograph Collection, North Carolina Office of Archives and History, Raleigh, N.C.

These unidentified flood scenes appear in a scrapbook created by Lincoln County resident Alfred Nixon. Courtesy of the Lincoln County Historical Association.

What appears to be a lumber yard is captured in this panorama of North Wilkesboro after the flood. It was taken by an unknown photographer from a point on E Street, approximately 400-500 feet east of 13th Street. Courtesy Finley Family Archives (private collection), Wilkesboro, N.C.

RIGHT: Jimmy Brown's house near Linville Falls post-flood. From the Frank W. Bicknell Photograph Collection, North Carolina Office of Archives and History, Raleigh, N.C.

LEFT: Heavy rain washed out this 120-foot tall fill containing 85,000 cubic yards of material from beneath the Southern Railway's line between Ridgecrest and Old Fort, leaving the track swinging. From *The Floods of 1916*, page 66.

Situated on a narrow strip of land between the French Broad River and steep hillsides to the north, the town of Marshall suffered devastating destruction and property loss. James Guthrie and Altha Briggs lost their lives attempting to salvage items from a café that stood in the vicinity of the depot, pictured here a few weeks after the flood. Guthrie's fifteen-year-old son Herman, who had witnessed his father's death and who himself had nearly drowned, was so devastated by the event that he caught the first train out of town three weeks later. From *The Floods of July 1916*, 77.

The flooding of the French Broad River in Asheville had a catastrophic impact on the industrial district and Riverside Park. ABOVE: This panorama by James M. McCanless of the flooded French Broad River in Asheville reveals what Fred A. Olds would have seen on his tour of the riverfront on July 16. The West Asheville Bridge, which stood until 1972, is the focal point of the image. RIGHT: Captured by William A. Barnhill, this image shows a streetcar barn at Riverside Park shortly after the flood. The floodwaters ripped off large portions of the barn's roof and nearly pushed the entire structure completely over, leaving it leaning at a severe angle when the water receded. Both images courtesy North Carolina Collection, Pack Memorial Library, Asheville, North Carolina.

Morganton residents gather on the edge of the flooded Catawba River along present-day North Green Street. Image from the Estate of Jean Conyers Ervin. It appears courtesy of Picture Burke, a digital photograph preservation project of the Burke County Public Library.

Seven-year-old Mabel Stepp visited the small town of Chimney Rock just one week after the flood. In 1986, she recalled the devastation: "Broad River had washed away to nothing but a trickle running over some rocks. The houses were wrecked, there was debris hanging in the trees. It looked just like a tornado hit." Severe erosion contributed to the apocalyptic scene. The stacked stone wall of this well near Chimney Rock was left completely exposed after floodwaters washed away twelve feet of soil. From *The Floods of July 1916*, 24.

When the floodwaters receded, North Carolinians all over the flood district very quickly undertook the monumental task of rebuilding. Some companies, like the Southern Railway and Southern Power Company, mobilized on a massive scale and had much of their damaged infrastructure fixed within months. Others had suffered such a financial blow that they determined not to rebuild. For this reason, the mill communities of West Monbo and Mountain Island exist only in the memories of those who once lived and worked there. At Old Fort, citizens posed for this photograph with shovels and pick axes in hand during their recovery effort. Courtesy Mountain Gateway Museum, Old Fort, N.C.

Index

www.ingramcontent.com/pod-product-compliance
Lightning Source LLC
Chambersburg PA
CBHW040903030225
R16175000001B/R161750PG21256CBX00027B/3

9780865264816